Home Production of Poultry and Eggs

by The Willowbrook Company

with an introduction by Jackson Chambers

Self Reliance Books

Get more historic titles on animal and stock breeding, gardening and old fashioned skills by visiting us at:

http://selfreliancebooks.blogspot.com/

Introduction

I am pleased to present yet another title on Poultry.

This volume is entitled "Home Production of Poultry and Eggs" and was published in 1910.

The work is in the Public Domain and is re-printed here in accordance with Federal Laws.

As with all reprinted books of this age that are intended to perfectly reproduce the original edition, considerable pains and effort had to be undertaken to correct fading and sometimes outright damage to existing proofs of this title. At times, this task is quite monumental, requiring an almost total "rebuilding" of some pages from digital proofs of multiple copies. Despite this, imperfections still sometimes exist in the final proof and may detract from the visual appearance of the text.

I hope you enjoy reading this book as much as I enjoyed making it available to readers again.

Jackson Chambers

Kellerstrass Farm

Arthur Oscar Schilling
1907

1

CONTENTS

THE INTRODUCTION

IT IS not alone the Price, but the extreme difficulty so often experienced in buying Real Fresh Eggs and Properly Conditioned Poultry, that has caused many people to go into the business on a scale just commensurate with their own Family Needs, and it is for the thousands of others who can readily follow their lead that this Booklet has been prepared.

To put you in the way of having your table supplied with better than "The Best The Market Affords" and at a Less Cost, is surely something that you can but appreciate, and when you find how easy it is you will regret that you have never taken it up before.

It is a fact that a great many people have been unsuccessful in Raising Poultry, and to that fact must be attributed, more perhaps than to any other, the Exhorbitant Prices which now prevail for so great a part of each year for all kinds of Poultry Products, and as the tendency is constantly upward, the situation is one that is justly the cause of Grave Apprehension. If nothing is done to counteract this tendency Poultry and Eggs will soon become Articles of Food which only the rich can afford, and in view of such conditions it is apparent that the people themselves must take the matter up, find out wherein the trouble lies and determine on some plan for its correction.

It is entirely safe to say that the majority of people who fail in any business do so because of one of two reasons; either they are temperamentally unfitted for the business or else, having the natural qualifications necessary, their Education and Training has been along improper and erroneous lines, and it must be apparent that these two things are just as much a factor in Poultry Culture as in any thing else. The majority of people have in them enough of natural attributes, in spite of the artificiality of modern life, to enable them to cope with a process that is, in itself, primarily natural, and succeed if they are properly instructed in the beginning. The Great Things of Life, without exception, have had their Inception in Small Beginnings and have only become Large by a Natural Growth.

THE WILLOWBROOK WAY

There are thousands of people who can take up Poultry Culture for the purpose of supplying their own Needs and protecting themselves from the exorbitant prices now prevailing, and, being properly founded, succeed in Accomplishing that Result, and many of them, using their Experience so gained as a basis, can go on, building up gradually and little by little and finally develop a Commercial Proposition that will bring them Splendid Returns.

With such people in mind this Booklet has been compiled in order that they may have a simple, direct and well arranged guide to get them Started Right. In it only General Principles are dealt with, for the reason that a full and comprehensive knowledge of such principles can best be given if they stand out by themselves, free from a thousand and one details which only tend to obscure and cloud the Basic Truths that are so necessary to have clearly set forth and absorbed as a Foundation for Future Growth.

There are many works published treating of the question in hand, some abounding in the revelation of so called "poultry secrets" held out as being the magic wand which has only to be waved over your flock to produce the most astounding results, and others, excellent in their way, which attempt to cover and provide for each and every possible contingency that may arise for all time, and in the doing of which the facts so necessary and essential to the beginner are hopelessly intermingled with a mass of subjects of no use or interest whatever to him at the time. The natural and almost necessary result is that in attempting to cull out what he needs he becomes confused and does not get a proper and comprehensive grasp of the Prime Essentials.

In "The Willowbrook Way" there are no "wonderful magic secrets" and only such features are dealt with as have been proven by experience to be of Practical Use to the beginner, and these are set forth in such direct, well ordered and simple form that no one who will follow them can go far wrong in his or her undertaking.

You will readily infer from the above that the suggested answer to the problem presented is this: "Raise your own Poultry, Produce your own Eggs, Save Money in doing so and then, if you have the Inclination, turn the Knowledge gained in the Process to a source of Profit by gradually expanding and putting your business on a Prosperous Commercial Basis and do it all by "The Willowbrook Way."

It is, as has been stated above, impossible to foresee and provide in the first instance for all Questions of Detail in any Business or Undertaking. It must first be Properly Started and then its needs provided for as they arise, and for the purpose of assisting you in matters which, for the reasons heretofore given, have purposely been omitted from this work, a Plan has been devised, whereby for a fee barely sufficient to cover actual cost, you can at any time secure information and advice as to any Particular Question, Trouble or Item of Detail that may confront you. This you will find outlined in full in folder enclosed and your particular attention is invited to it.

THE HOUSE.

THE House should front to the south and should have a Substantial Foundation of Concrete, or Stone laid with cement, extending at least two feet below the level of the ground. It should be large enough so that each fowl will have from three and one-half to four square feet of floor space, and the Yard, or Run, should be, within reasonable limits, as large as possible, but where available space is limited, a very small run, if kept clean and worked over often, will suffice. Many people succeed with no run at all and it is undoubtedly a Practical Proposition to successfully handle fowls which are constantly and continuously housed. Where, however, a run can be had, it would be folly to ignore the Benefits which the fowls will derive from its use.

The Essentials in the house are Dryness, Ventillation, Light, Warmth and total absence of Drafts. The Floor is all important and if the Ground is used as such it should be sub-drained, and then only where the house is so located that the general grade and drainage is away from it. If Cement is used it should be put down in two layers with heavy tar paper between and be laid on a foundation of Gravel or Cinders. A Board Floor is good if it is tight, but a properly constructed Cement Floor is best of all.

DRYNESS will depend on the floor construction and drainage as outlined, together with proper ventilation which is treated of below.

VENTILATION is best provided by the use of Muslin Fronts, preferably on hinged frames so they can be opened in mild weather. The exact detail of these Fronts is immaterial, but they should occupy fully one-third of the house front and are preferably arranged in sections so that different degrees of ventilation can be obtained by opening a greater or less portion of the front in accordance with the weather conditions. The better arrangement, it is believed, is to have two narrow panels, or curtains, extend well across the front near the top, and another and broader one to occupy practically all the space between the window and the side of the house. This arrangement is clearly indicated in the Cut showing the

House Front and the best results will be obtained by following it closely.

LIGHT should be admitted through a Window, not necessarily wide, but extending nearly from the bottom to the top of the house front so that the Sun's Rays will reach, as nearly as possible, the Entire Interior.

WARMTH is obtained by proper construction, as outlined below, together with the exercise of Extreme Care in so making the plans that the interior height is kept at the lowest point consistent with comfortable use.

DRAFTS are to be absolutely eliminated. Have all the air possible admitted from the front, but the Floor, Sides, Back and Roof must be, as nearly as they can be made, air proof. The material used in the house is not important so long as these results are reached, and a house can be built of almost any Odds and Ends by using tar or building paper or light sheet roofing for the purpose of making it Tight and Warm. In the colder climates it is advisable to have the outer walls double and in that case the paper should be placed between the two thicknesses of lumber.

If Extra Warmth is indicated by Climate or Location the walls and roof can be reinforced by sheathing on the inside of the posts and rafters, thus leaving an air space or chamber between the outer and inner walls and adding greatly to their cold-resisting properties. This space is sometimes filled with sawdust or other insulating material, but that method is not here recommended as the filling is liable to gather moisture and make the house damp.

The latest and Best Plan for guarding against Drafts and bettering the Ventilation is to have the Rear Studding sheathed from the Rafters down to a point below the Dropping Board and the Sheathing continued on the Rafters to a point about one foot beyond the front line of the Dropping Board. By doing this and leaving the Air Space so created open at the top and bottom a circulation of the Air admitted through the Curtain Fronts is obtained which absolutely and effectively draws out all Dampness and keeps the air Dry and Pure.

The Attached Plans are easily understood and houses built after them will readily accommodate the number of fowls indicated, and the one corresponding with the Smaller Dimensions will not be too large for a less number than specified if so many are not needed.

A very Common Error is that of building the house too high, and this is to be specially guarded against in those sections where the winters are severe. It should be high enough simply to permit the necessary inside work to be done easily. Anything over that is excess space and tends to make the house colder in winter. (See note.)

The Dimensions indicated in connection with the Index to Plans will well care for the average needs and will provide a home for your fowls where they will be Comfortable, Happy and Productive no matter what the weather may be provided always you give them proper care.

The Windows and Lower Curtain Fronts should be hung from the top and arranged to swing up under the roof inside. This permits the open-

Note—If you already have such a house the defect can be to a great extent overcome by having a burlap or muslin curtain arranged to drop down in front of the roosts at night, or by providing the interior sheathing system of ventilation as described above.

ing being covered with Wire Netting outside to not only keep the fowls in but to prevent the entrance of skunks and other destructive enemies. The Upper Curtain Fronts should be hung from the top also but arranged to swing out so they can be utilized as Awnings in hot weather.

THE HOUSE EQUIPMENT.

A GALVANIZED Water Fountain can be purchased for seventy-five cents and the Feed Hoppers can be made from any thin lumber, or they can be obtained from dealers in poultry supplies at a small cost. They can be made or purchased with one or more compartments and for an ordinary pen but two are necessary. One of these should have three compartments and be used for Grit, Oyster Shells and Charcoal and the other should be single and given up to the Dry Mash. The Nests—and there should be six of them—must be enclosed in front, leaving an opening just large enough for the hens to get in and out. In large houses, where there are several pens, an alley-way, or passage, is often provided, extending the full length of the house and in rear of the pens. With this arrangement the nests are located under the dropping board with an adjustable opening into the passage so the eggs can be gathered with-out going into the pens, but with a single house, as here described, they are best placed along the side opposite the door, or on a Shelf under the dropping board, so the front of the Nests will be even with the front of the board, and a hinged drop should be provided to close up the front of the nests. This compels the fowls to enter from the rear, giving them a Secluded Place in which to lay, and at the same time enables you to gather the eggs by simply opening the hinged drop. The Shelf on which the Nests rest should extend some six inches beyond the back of the boxes, thus affording the fowls an easy manner of entrance.

The Roosts, or Perches, should be not less than one-and-three-quarter inches square with the upper side worked off to a half round and should be at least one foot above the dropping board. The Dropping Board, Roosts and Nests should rest upon cleats or brackets so they can be easily removed for cleaning. It is desirable when you want to produce eggs for hatching to have a coop attached to one of the side walls in which to keep the roosters when not running with the hens. This should be provided with Water and Feed Appliances and is best constructed with a solid bottom and slatted sides and top. It should be fastened to the wall at least three feet above the floor.

THE YARD OR RUN.

THE Yard or Run should be laid out as indicated above, in accordance with the space at your disposal, and be enclosed with Wire Netting, or, better still, Galvanized Poultry Fence. A board six inches wide should be set into the ground two inches and connect the bottoms of the posts, and the lower edge of the netting or fence secured to it with staples. Nothing in the way of a rail should be placed at the top. A Gate should be provided in the Yard Fence for easy access in cleaning and summer feeding. The Side Door in the house may be omitted and entrance made through the yard gate and the front door if desired, but the side house door is strongly recommended as it will be found not only a great convenience but a time saver as well.

In locating the House the matter of the Run should receive attention. The ground to be devoted to it should, if possible, slope away from the house and should be well drained so it will not retain moisture and become damp and soggy. Dryness in the Run is of almost equal importance with Dryness in the House. The soil should be fertile and every effort should be made to keep it seeded. The fowls will scratch and dig it up and in so doing derive much benefit which they would not obtain if the ground were bare, and it is therefore of much importance that this recommendation be carried out as far as is possible, and if the area of the run is sufficient there will be little trouble in keeping some part of it under seed at all times.

THE STOCK.

HAVING your House Erected and Equipped as described you come to the question of Stock and you have to decide not only how many hens you will require for your use, but what kind or breed will best suit your purposes or needs, and also, how you can best obtain what you finally determine you want. In deciding the first question you can safely figure that hens coming from Good Strong Stock, and given proper treatment and attention, will lay, as a minimum, one egg each every other day, or, as a concrete proposition, a pen of twelve such hens should produce a minimum average of six eggs per day during their laying season. This is putting it on a conservative basis, for with the improvement which is constantly taking place in breeding and raising chickens the average egg production per fowl is steadily increasing; many poultrymen are getting an average much in excess of that named and the statement is freely made that the "two hundred egg per year hen" has arrived and is very much in evidence, and it is an admitted fact that hens have been made to produce 240 eggs each per year.

For Domestic Uses what is known as General Utility Fowls are best. The commercial poultryman many times raise and keep several different breeds; one, for example, for Egg Producers, another for Early Broilers and Market Uses, and perhaps still another for Show and Advertising Purposes, but the fowl that will combine the two first mentioned qualifications will best answer private and domestic needs. In other words, a breed which will produce a good fair average output of eggs and at the same time mature early and grow to a size which makes them available for the table, answers the title above given, i. e., A General Utility Fowl. Our own First Choice to answer these conditions would be the WHITE WYANDOTTES, but other varieties of Wyandottes, Minorcas, Orphingtons, Plymouth Rocks and Rhode Island Reds all have their advocates and all comply, to a greater or less extent, with the requirements outlined above. If you should decide, however, that you only want your chickens for their Egg Producing Capacity, there is but little question but that the Leghorns are Leaders in that line; in fact they are rapidly becoming known as the "Egg Machines." If you are so located that you have personal access to well reputed poultrymen, your better plan will be to look over the different varieties, get all the information you can as to their laying qualities, and select the breed or strain that you then feel will suit you best. If, however, such opportunity is not open to you, the advertisements in any reliable Poultry Paper—and there are many such—will serve as a guide and enable you to make a satisfactory selection and obtain the stock you need. Questions of Hatching, Incubation, Breeding, etc., do not apply to the proposition in hand and you have simply to buy the stock you decide on, put them in the quarters you have prepared, and if they are as represented, active, well bred, laying fowls, you should begin gathering eggs as soon as they become accustomed to their new home. Early Hatched Spring Pullets should be procured unless you are buying your stock in the spring, when you would, of course, want Yearlings or hens hatched the previous Season. After your hens, so procured, have laid through the year they should be killed off and replaced by New Stock. If, however, you conclude the second spring to raise a few chickens yourself, keep the "Old Hens" for that purpose. Their eggs will produce Stronger and Better Stock than those of the pullets, they will set more consistently and brood their chickens more carefully. Unless you wish to raise chickens you will not require a rooster nor will you need the small coop mentioned in connection with the description of the house. Pullets and hens lay as well, and many claim better, where they are not running with the cocks and they should never be turned together until a short time before it is intended to save the eggs for hatching. The pro_duction of eggs for hatching, their incubation and the raising of chicks is a subject foreign to that of this book, but one that we will be glad to take up with you at any time when you think it will be of interest and benefit to you.

THE FEEDING.

NOW that you have your hens safely installed in their new home they must be fed and cared for, and here is where the intuitive knowledge of the Natural Poultryman comes in play. No matter how fine and well arranged the quarters or how well bred the stock, they will amount to but little without proper food and care. The Feeding Problem is, however, greatly simplified in case of a small number of fowls, for the Refuse and Waste from the Table of an ordinary family will go a long ways toward providing their food, and it is freely admitted by nearly everyone who has made a study of the subject that nothing better than this same waste can be obtained. Some grain must, of course, be given them and they should have all the Oyster Shells, Charcoal and Grit that they will eat. The Oyster Shells, Charcoal and Grit should always be before them, preferably in hoppers, and a hopper filled with a Dry Mash will be relished by the fowls and aid materially in their Egg Production and at the same time lessen to some extent the labor items involved in their care. Cut Green Bone and Fresh Meat Scraps are also desirable items of feed, and a Head of Cabbage suspended from the rafters by a cord or wire, just high enough to compel the hens to jump off the floor in order to get at it, serves the double purpose of affording them a much needed Green Vegetable Diet and an equally Much Needed Exercise. Among the Grains which are available may be mentioned Wheat, Barley, Oats, Buckwheat, Cracked Corn, Corn Meal, Wheat Middlings and Wheat Bran.

This tells you in a general way the Needs of the Fowls and what is available to satisfy those needs. Just what shall be used, how much of each and when, are problems that you must, within certain limitations, work out for yourself. It must be borne in mind, however, from the outset, that more hens are ruined, so far as their egg production is concerned, by over-feeding than by the reverse. Over-feeding not only makes a hen lazy—and a lazy hen will not lay— but it tends to the accumulation of so much Fat around the Egg Producing Organs that their Functions are seriously Impeded if not Totally

Impaired. A common sense rule is this: If, when you go into the pen with a pan of feed, your hens do not rush up to you and show unmistakable signs of being hungry, don't feed them, for they do not want it and consequently are better off without it.

As a Guide in this matter of Diet the following will be of use but it can, of course, be changed and modified to suit conditions and requirements. Keep before them at all times Hoppers of Oyster Shells, Grit, Charcoal and Dry Mash. (a) Give them Scratch Food (b) scattered over the

(a) An Approved Formula for Dry Mash and one which is highly recommended by the Department at Cornell University is the following: Six parts each of Corn Meal and Wheat Middlings, Five parts of fine Beef Scraps, Three parts of Wheat Bran, One part of Alfalfa Meal and One part of Old Process Linseed Oil Meal. Cut Green Clover can be used instead of Alfalfa Meal but it does not contain as much nutrition and is in consequence not as good.

(b) This may consist of a mixture, in equal parts, of such grains as you have on hand, or, better still, of the same grains cracked and mixed. If you have to procure grain especially for this purpose good clean wheat and cracked corn in equal parts should be used. The market offers many scratch foods which contain other ingredients than the above, but if your pen is always supplied with the hopper foods suggested, this mixture will answer every purpose.

Litter in the morning and again just before dark in the afternoon.

Give them a head of Cabbage or a Mangel, suspended as before mentioned, every day or two. When it is possible give them all the Milk they will drink. Skim Milk is good and Sour Milk boiled until it curds is also excellent. A much relished and valuable Winter Green Food is Sprouted Oats. This is prepared by putting a layer of oats about one inch thick in a flat box or tub, placing the box or tub in the lightest part of the cellar or behind the kitchen range, and wetting the oats thoroughly every day. They will Start Quickly and in a very short time the Green Sprouts will have acquired a very considerable size. Pieces can then be broken off the mass and given to the fowls in connection with their Other Feed. This should be prepared only in such quantities as will admit of its being used as soon as it is ready, for if it is allowed to stand after the sprouts have acquired a growth of more than an inch the Nutritive Qualities are taken up and carried off by the atmosphere.

In this Method of Feeding the Wet Mash so

much in vogue in days gone by is eliminated and, with it, about one-half of the Labor formerly required is done away with. In order to make the method successful much judgment must be used and the fowls must be forced to eat the Dry Mash. They will naturally choose the Grain Ration and, to make them eat properly, the Morning Feed of Scratch Grain must be very light and only sufficient to force them to take a sufficient amount of Early Exercise to get their Organs in Proper Operation. They will then eat the Dry Mash from the Hopper during the day and eat only such an amount as they actually require and be ready for their Evening Scratch Food when it comes time to give it to them.

Last, but by no means least, they must have Clean, Fresh Water at all times and in winter the Water Fountains should be filled two or three times a day with Warm Water.

A Plan, much practiced and a good one too, is to throw in the Morning Feed of Scratch Grain after dark the night before. When this is done the hens will begin scratching for it as soon as it is light and so get a lot of early and valuable exercise which they otherwise would not have.

With these Suggestions and Rules in mind you can, by watching and studying your fowls, ascertain their Special Needs and Requirements and so arrange and manage their Feeding as to keep them in Proper Condition for the Service you expect from them.

This Feeding matter sounds complicated and formidable as you read it, but a little experience will show you that it is, on the contrary, extremely simple, and only seems otherwise because of the variety of stuff which may be utilized. While it is all Useful it does not follow that every bit of it is Absolutely Necessary, and, aside from those items which have been mentioned in mandatory terms, like the Grit, Charcoal, Oyster Shells, Dry Mash, Green Food and Water, you can safely use only such of the others as you can readily obtain and not be apprehensive as to the results.

THE GENERAL CARE.

YOU now have your Plant in operation and the question of Care and Housekeeping comes in. Cleanliness is the First Essential. The Nests should have Fresh, Clean Straw in them at all times. The Floor, when the hens are kept in on account of the weather, should be covered with a Litter of Straw or Dry Leaves four or five inches thick and this should be renewed from time to time as it gets foul and dirty. The Roosts should be kept clean and brushed over with kerosene oil every few days. The Dropping Board should have a thin coating of Sawdust, Dry Sand or Fine Dirt to keep the droppings from fouling it and the droppings should be removed every day. The Feed Hoppers should be kept clean and a sharply beveled cover upon which the fowls cannot roost will aid materially in accomplishing this. The Water Fountains should be scalded out with boiling water at frequent intervals, for a chicken is as much dependent for health upon clean, pure drinking water as is a human being. The Whole Interior should be

Whitewashed at least twice a year, in the spring and fall, and particular care must be exercised to see that the Whitewash is forced into all the cracks and corners.

. The Windows and Muslin Fronts must be adjusted according to weather conditions, the object being to give the fowls plenty of good fresh air without allowing Rain, Snow or Dampness to penetrate the Interior of the House. The hens should be given the Freedom of the Yard during pleasant weather but must not be allowed outside when there is snow or ice on the ground.

THE CONCLUSION.

THE Above, it is believed, covers in a General Way, and yet sufficiently in detail, the proposition of Handling Poultry on a small scale for Family and Domestic Needs, to enable the average person to follow it out to a Successful Conclusion, and place him or herself in a position where they can not only provide themselves and their families with an ample and absolutely Reliable Supply of the best food product known to modern science, but can do so at a Less Cost than the Market Price of the same product of an unknown but usually inferior quality.

If you care, after trying this plan for a time, to extend your operations and take up poultry as a Commercial Proposition the foregoing will all be of use, as the same general rules apply to all plants, whether large or small, and while this work is intended only as a Guide for the Small Domestic Producer, it will not be without Value to the person who goes into the business on a large scale.

No mention has been made of Diseases and their Treatment, for it is believed that the best treatment is Prevention, and if the spirit of the foregoing is carried into effect Troubles of that kind will be conspicuous by their absence.

"The Willowbrook Way," while an economizer of expenditure, space and labor, is prolific in Results, and those of its many readers and students who follow it carefully and consciencciously will in no wise be disappointed at the outcome.

You will find that all General Questions have been fully dealt with and the ordinary routine of domestic poultry culture fully covered. If it becomes necessary for you to obtain any Specific Information or Advice in the future you can be assured that by using the means heretofore referred to your Special Questions will be handled in a manner which will be equally intelligent and satisfactory.

THE WILLOWBROOK WAY

INDEX TO PLANS

(See Pages 35-36.)

Figure 1—Front Elevation.

Figure 2—Ground Plan.

Figure 3—Perspective, showing arrangement of Dropping Boards and Roosts.

Figure 4—Method of erecting Yard Fence.

Figure 5—Feed Hopper.

Figure 6—Nest Boxes.

Details in each of these figures are indicated by letters as follows: A—Muslin Fronts. B—Doors C—Windows. D—Dropping Boards. E—Roosts or Perches. F—Water Fountain. G—Feed Hoppers. H—Nests. I—Posts for Fence. K—Board to which bottom of Fence is attached.

For 20 fowls build this house 10 feet long and 8 feet wide, with posts 6½ feet in front and 5 feet in rear.

For 30 fowls make the ground size 12 feet by 10 feet and height same as above.

Don't keep more than 30 fowls in a single Pen or House.

THE WILLOWBROOK WAY

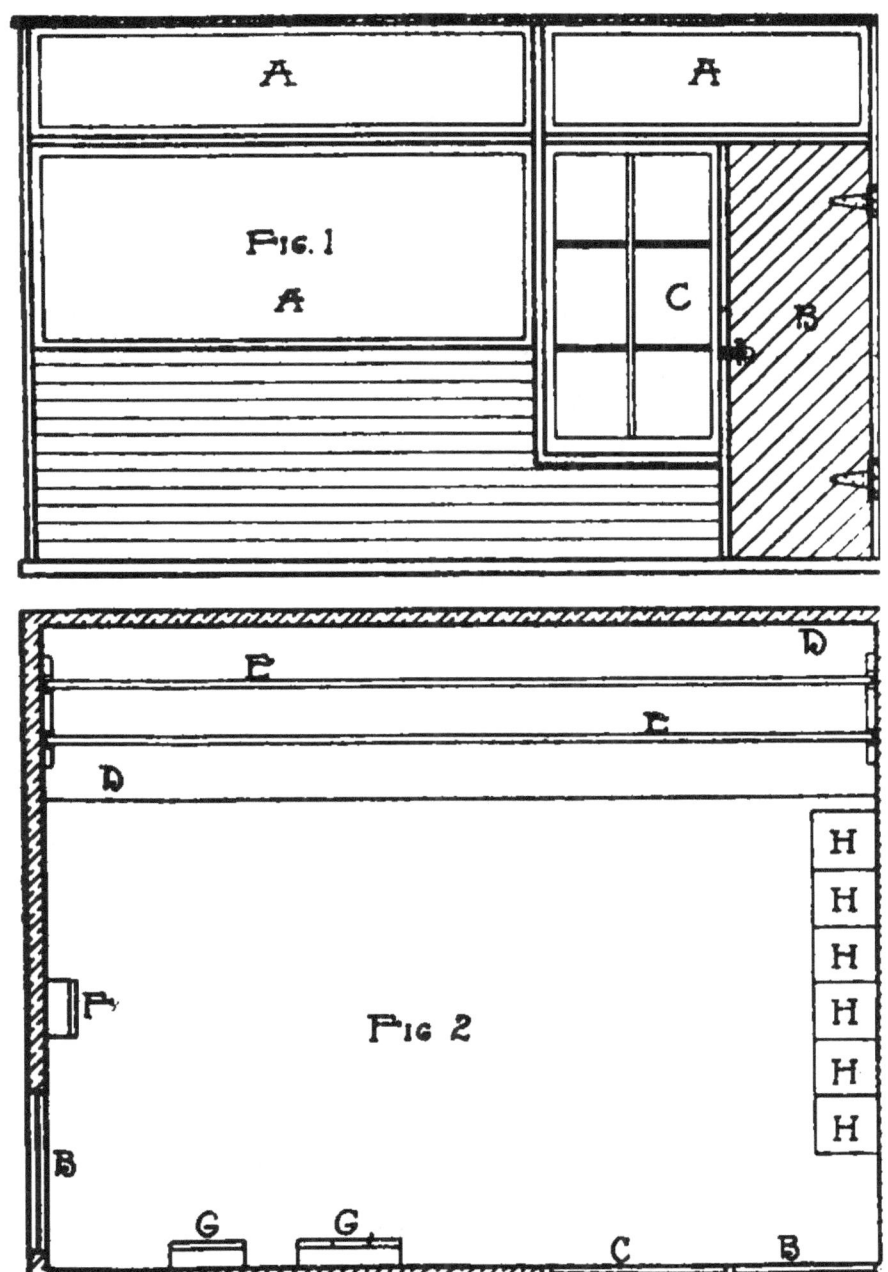

THE WILLOWBROOK WAY

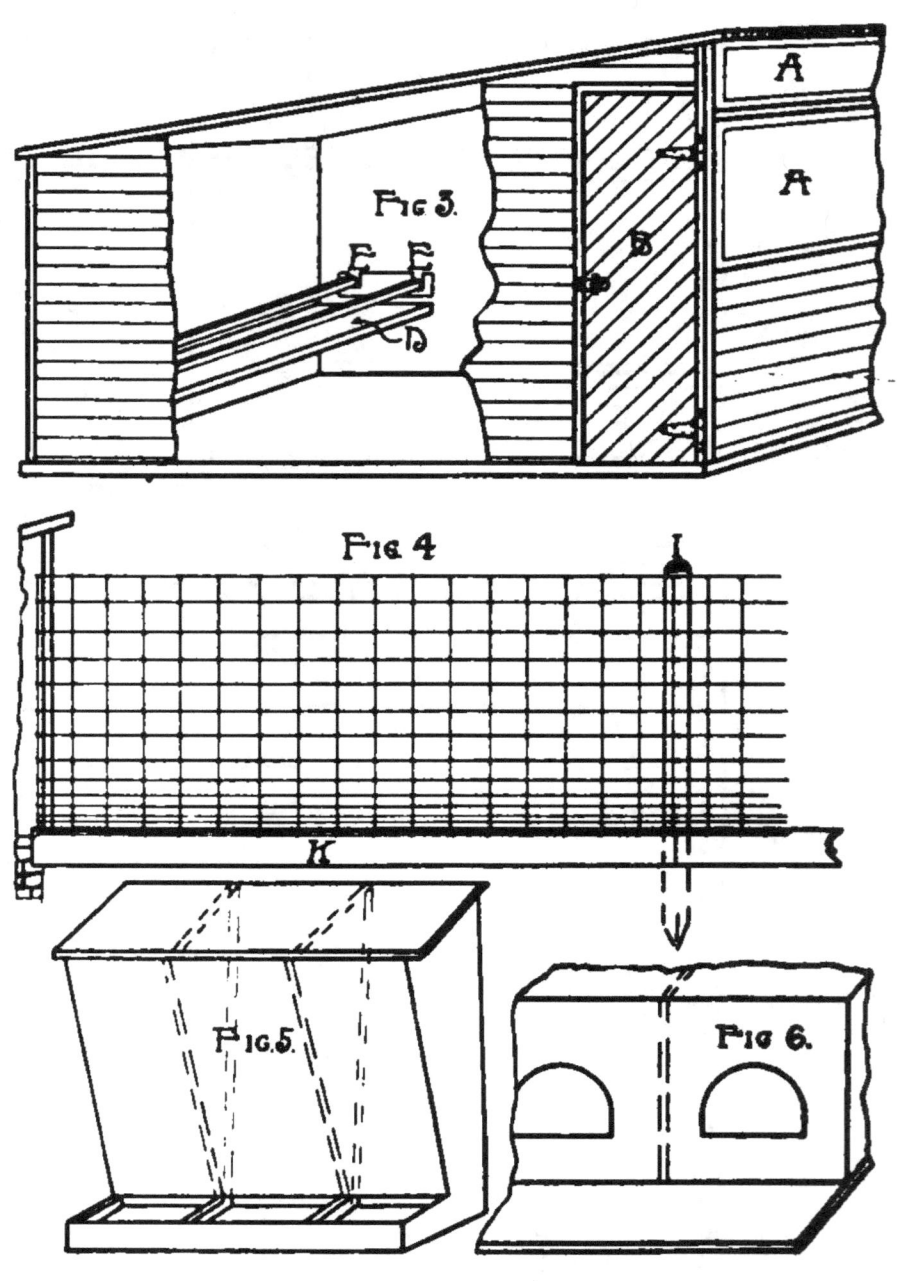

Fig 3.

Fig 4.

Fig 5.

Fig 6.

www.ingramcontent.com/pod-product-compliance
Lightning Source LLC
Chambersburg PA
CBHW081126280526
45787CB00007B/3000